BRANDYWINE BOY

ADRIAN R. MORRISON

ILLUSTRATIONS BY GAYLE JOSEPH

ISBN: 1480223212
ISBN-13: 9781480223219

DEDICATION

To my wife, Olive, with love and appreciation,
another payment on a debt that can never be fully repaid

ACKNOWLEDGMENTS

As I wrote in *An Odyssey with Animals,* "The chance to thank friends and colleagues for their generous assistance as I wrote this book was the best part of all—after the Dedication."

I thank Gayle Joseph, of course, for her marvelous illustrations. She shared my enthusiasm for the project.

The excellent staff of the Steven W. Atwood Library of the School of Veterinary Medicine, University of Pennsylvania— Margy Lindem, Frank Campbell, Catherine Hinton, Karen Lash, and Becca Lausch— were of considerable assistance to me over the past few years.

John Aaron— fellow member of Captain Midnight's Secret Squadron; classmate at Chadds Ford School; Kennett High School; Franklin and Marshall College; and fraternity brother— proved invaluable in recollecting Chadds Ford village and its inhabitants, including Andrew Wyeth and Chris Sanderson. John is now a docent at the Chris Sanderson Museum. It was great fun to return to our collaboration as Secret Squadron members.

Lois Sands, former Chadds Ford and Kennett classmate, also lived in the village. She is a retired elementary school teacher and now a docent at the Brandywine River Museum. She, too, was a big help with village and school memories

Kennett High School classmate, Nancy Haldeman, assisted me with her knowledge of the present-day Chadds Ford area and its inhabitants.

Wanda Kevis, Harry Kevis's widow and Kennett High classmate, helped me with the Snack Shack memories and her appreciation of the humor in the book.

I also thank Mary Landa, the Wyeth Collection Manager, for information on Andrew Wyeth's models.

J. R. Alden's *The American Revolution: 1775–1783*, published by Harper and Brothers, New York in 1954, provided details of the Battle of the Brandywine. Our version of *The Scottish Chiefs* was published by Scribner's, New York in 1921. Other historical information also came from anonymous sources on the Internet.

The passage ending chapter six is quoted from Mary O'Hara's *My Friend Flicka*, published by Lippencott in 1941, pp. 50–51.

Information on Squire Cheney came from an article by Susannah Brody, "Squire Thomas Cheney, Patriot, Farmer and Judge," *Chester County Day*, October 6, 2012.

My former classmates saved me from myself more than once, just as did the anonymous reviewers of my earlier book, *An Odyssey with Animals*. As far as I know, errors of fact would be mine.

TABLE OF CONTENTS

PREFACE

Love, Grandad was the original title of this book because our daughter, Ellen, asked if I would write the stories I had told her about growing up on a small farm just twenty-five miles from Philadelphia. She wanted her two children to learn what life was like outside suburbia, where they are growing up. Naturally, the stories speak of a quite different era—more than sixty years ago. They begin during the closing years of World War II, 1944 and 1945, and end in the summer of 1953. That is just nine years, but those years were packed with adventure. Of course my six other grandchildren were part of my intended audience as well.

As I wrote, I realized that others might also enjoy my stories, particularly teenagers who pick up this book. Also, there are stories suitable for reading to younger children. As I have learned from friends who have read the manuscript, the stories also interest adults of my generation; my experiences have evoked memories in the minds of my friends. The book will have particular interest for those who know something of the history of the pastoral Brandywine Valley and its surrounding hills, where the Brandywine Creek courses from southeastern Pennsylvania to empty into the Christina River, which then flows into the Delaware River at Wilmington, Delaware.

The valley and the village of Chadds Ford, which lies just north of Brandywine Creek, were the site of a famous battle that pitted the colonials against the British and Hessian soldiers. The British nearly captured George Washington there! Also, the famous family of artists including N. C., Andrew, and Jamie Wyeth, made their home in the valley. Although I didn't know the Wyeths personally, I went to school with one of their models. We'll meet them and learn more of the Battle of the Brandywine later in the book.

In *Brandywine Boy*, you will also read of my wild ride when I jumped a barbed-wire gate with my horse while riding bareback. Another adventure was my felling of trees as a young boy in order to build a log cabin with three friends. Then there are the stories of the bombardier chicken; the pigeon I raised, taught to fly, and then released into the wild; and the time I had to drink from a swamp. These and other stories of my adventures pepper the book. They are not unlike those adventures of Tom Sawyer that Mark Twain told.

I am blessed with an extraordinary visual memory—which is probably why I became an anatomist and not a physicist—so that I was able to paint a vivid picture with words. Then my artist friend, Gayle Joseph, accurately transformed my memories into very nice illustrations.

Life was quite different from today in the early postwar years. Imagine having no television to watch. How did we survive? As you will learn, we did quite well exercising our imaginations while listening to the radio.

Being a veterinarian, I am naturally interested in how animal bodies work. I'll tell you a few interesting things along those lines as I speak of farms of sixty years ago and some of the ways they differ from those of today.

As I wrote for a wider audience, I realized that I wanted readers to see the magical creature that one might call Every Boy—the rural boys of my generation—as a Tom Sawyer of sorts. Of course the stories Every Boy might tell would differ in detail from those in this book, but they would contain some of the same elements of adventure and magic. I hope girls, with their own magical qualities, will read the stories, too, if only to gain insight into what makes the young rascals tick.

Additionally, I hope those adults who read this book might consider it to be a handbook for understanding energetic, sometimes mischievous boys. Speaking as both a father of four boys and a former scoutmaster, I believe that it will help.

CHAPTER 1

THE FARM

One Sunday afternoon in 1961, I recognized how important my family's small farm and the village of Chadds Ford, only one mile away in the Brandywine Valley, had been to me. After a combined eight years of study at college in Lancaster and then veterinary school at Cornell in New York, I returned to live just twelve miles from the farm with my wife and two small sons. I thought it would be a temporary stop while I studied for a PhD at the University of Pennsylvania before moving on to a permanent job elsewhere. The latter never happened. Instead I spent my career in one of the greatest veterinary schools and neuroscience centers in the world.

On that Sunday afternoon, I said to my wife, "Let's take a drive out to Chadds Ford." As we crested the hill on Baltimore Pike (Route 1) leading down into the Brandywine Valley and the village of Chadds Ford, I saw the familiar soft green of the wooded hills surrounding the valley and knew I was home. For the first time, I recognized that Chadds Ford, the Brandywine Creek, and my memory of the farm were in my soul. I can remember the scene and the feeling I had even though I experienced it more than fifty years ago. As I struggled to develop my career and provide for my family, Sunday trips to the Valley were soothing.

My family moved to Maplevale Farm in the summer of 1944 from Norwood, a suburb of my birthplace, Philadelphia, when I was eight years old and my brother, David, was a few months old. My father wanted to be near his aging parents and his badly crippled younger sister, Jean, who was ten years older than I. The idea was that my father would run the farm until his younger brother returned from the merchant marine to help him. Sadly, my Uncle Doug was killed not long after the move, so that dream never materialized. It wouldn't have worked anyway because agriculture began to change dramatically into big business after the war, and it would have taken more than our fifty-two acres and thirty milking cows to make a go of it. Thus, my father had to settle for a part-time farm.

Although I spent only nine years of my life on Maplevale Farm, it is still home in my heart. The farm or, more accurately, the experiences and people that entered my life made me what I am now to a considerable extent. My parents played the most important role in forming me, of course, but the farm was always there in the background. Thus, it is a major character in these stories.

The farm, no longer mine legally because we had to sell it in 1953 just after I graduated from high school, is still there as I left it—but only in my mind. Now, in reality, it is divided into the several plots of land we had to sell, and the pasture across from the barn is polluted by overly large houses. Still, the farm is mine and remains unchanged in my memory.

Before continuing with the stories I want to tell, I'll place the farm in relation to the village of Chadds Ford and the Brandywine Creek. A small creek enters the much larger Brandywine Creek just beyond my school, which lies across the Brandywine from Chadds Ford. If you follow the small creek upstream south, you will leave Baltimore Pike (US route 1) about one-half mile from Chadds Ford as the creek bed veers left to enter a side valley that was the center of so much of my fun. On the left of the creek a high hill rises rather steeply.

Farther on in the valley sits a large cow barn on the farm next to ours, no longer in use when I arrived. This is where three friends and I spent some Saturday afternoons playing train in the manure bucket that hung from an overhead track that intersected with other tracks. The switches permitted a rather long ride if one of us was adept at pulling the right lever to make the switches from track to track as one boy pushed another sitting in the bucket. Thankfully long unused by the time my friends and I came along, the bucket had been there to receive manure shoveled from the gutter behind where a row of cows would stand to be milked. The manure bucket moved along the track at a slower rate than it did with us in it and was ultimately emptied outside the barn.

The big hill to the left of the creek used to have a dirt road at the crest running for more than a quarter mile, just right for gallops on a horse. Sadly, trees and houses now cover the hill. The big barn later enjoyed about ten years as a ski lodge for Chadds Peak, where the wooded part of the hill served as a ski slope with a rope tow. This was not much of a ski area considering that we used to sled on the non-wooded section, although we did refer to it as Suicide Hill. We used Suicide Hill only when we felt particularly daring and the snow was deep enough to carry us over the large tufts of meadow grass.

A bit farther on, a dirt road, carried over the creek by a wooden bridge, began at Farmer John's house about a quarter mile to the left and ran about one hundred yards beyond the bridge to the boundary of our farm. The road then climbed steeply to reach our barn where it turned into the macadam road that still runs past our house, the spring house, and eventually up the hill to Baltimore Pike. At the top of the hill, I waited beside the road for the school bus and often marveled at the road sign that pointed to Baltimore eighty-two long miles to the south. Our family didn't travel very much in those days.

The man we always referred to as Farmer John is gone of course. His farm is now a housing development built on either side of the partly filled-in dirt road near his house. The rest of the road, once you near the creek, is filled in by dense brush. Now I can't get to the bridge that served as our diving platform into the wider part of the creek that was our swimming hole.

Before later owners ruined it with ugly additions, our house was a graceful building with a nice roofed veranda across the front and a side porch leading into the kitchen. Dating from 1806, the original simple stone building consisted of a cellar, a kitchen, and two little bedrooms on the third floor. The front portion of the house was then added later.

When we arrived in 1944, the kitchen had a primitive hand pump in the sink. Water reached the house from the springhouse about fifty yards up the road and was then pumped up into the kitchen. But my grandfather installed a pump in the cellar so we could have a more modern sink.

A word about springhouses: they also served as primitive refrigerators. Although we didn't use our springhouse as such, in times past perishables were kept in a trough through which the cold spring water ran.

Our garage was across the road, with the feed shed above it. Regrettably, that was where the coal bin was. As soon as I was strong enough to push a wheelbarrow filled with coal, it was up to me to get the coal to the bin in the cellar—no convenient oil deliveries for us. Heat was delivered from the furnace through pipes that opened into holes in the floor or registers, which consisted of iron gratings. Thanks to the fact that warm air rises, my bedroom on the second floor was heated via a register on its floor. In the winter, though, I really had to snuggle down in my bed to keep warm.

Also across the road from our house were steps leading up to higher ground, where various chicken coops and other outbuildings stood on about two acres. Beside the steps, in and behind the stone wall, were huge, fragrant lilac bushes. As a teenager I learned to rebuild rock walls without mortar because of various collapses of the old wall that occurred from time to time. Rebuilding a rock wall was like solving a three-dimensional puzzle; it was actually fun.

Not fun were the vegetable gardens, immense monsters that required endless weeding. They lay near the largest chicken house where we kept our laying hens. Beyond were about thirty acres of fields with a woodlot extending to the left as a dogleg from what we called the back pasture. The creek we swam in led to the woods, which served as our camping ground. This area was a major source of fun and the site of the log cabin my friends and I built as very young boys. The rest of the thirty acres sloped upward to the place we always referred to as High Point. From there we looked down over the farm toward Farmer John's and beyond to other green hills.

Our farm would have been almost a perfect square except for the approximately ten-acre parcel that indented it from the dirt road back to the dogleg. That property belonged to the family of Frank McFadden, my boyhood hero and friend. We bought Maple-vale Farm from Frank's grandmother. (Our house had a number of large maple trees in the yard that were removed some time after we left, leaving the house looking forlorn to me now.)

Frank, brothers Bob and Rod Russo, and I formed the group that shared in the adventures in my fifty-two-acre playground. Time didn't exist then. We went from day to day—with morning summer chores and then school interfering of course—roaming, camping, swimming, fighting, and dreaming. We packed so much fun into those years from when I arrived as an eight-year-old city boy to when I left very reluctantly at seventeen, leaving the farm and my childhood behind as we moved to Wisconsin because my father had been transferred there by his company. Leaving the farm that summer of 1953 was so hard on me that for at least two weeks I didn't speak to my father, whom I have come to love (in my memory) more and more as the years have passed. Indeed, it brought tears to my eyes just writing the previous sentence.

CHAPTER 2

THE WOODS

Our three playgrounds, other than the fields of the farm in general, were the woods, the barn, and the swimming hole. Although the time we spent in these places seemed endless, it lasted only about five years until Frank and Bob reached about sixteen, followed by Bob and Rod leaving our Chadds Ford School to go to Westtown School. Frank and I lost touch with the Russos; and Frank was approaching manhood, college, and the army. So at about fifteen, I felt suddenly alone on the farm. But those earlier years were full of adventures that only boys can dream up, and they are the stuff of this book. Because I ended the first chapter describing the farm by mentioning the wooded dogleg to the left in our property, I'll start with the woods, the most fun-filled place of all. When my family bought Maplevale Farm, the other boys then had free rein to play in the woods with me.

The trees of the woods were scattered and very tall as you started down the hill, but the woods thickened upon reaching flat ground and went on to the creek that ran through the woods, narrow enough in some places to jump across. On the other side of the creek, you faced a rather steep hill that ended at our property line before the woods properly ended. If you turned to go up the creek several yards, the bank of the creek widened. It was this area that became our campground and the place where we ultimately built a log cabin. I'll talk about that adventure later in this chapter. You'll be stunned by what four boys accomplished and amazed that our parents permitted us to do it.

We camped a lot during those summers, the first of which was when I was nine. Our first campout was not near the creek but in a clearing near the top of the hill. It also turned into something of a farce.

We started the night with a fire, over which we prepared what seemed to be our standard meal from then on: Vienna sausages and baked beans cooked in a scout pot. Marshmallows toasted on a stick were a common dessert. After eating we sat around the campfire telling tall stories and all the other imaginative things boys can come up with to talk about. Then we decided it must be time for bed. We had no tent or sleeping bags, just blankets folded over each other and held together with big blanket pins. To protect us from the dampness of the ground, we laid down a ground cloth. Our beds were the hard ground with some leaves piled on it under the ground cloth—no air mattresses or other pads in those days.

At some point, someone woke up and said it was time for breakfast. So we got up and made a fire to cook our eggs and bacon. Then we packed up, including the dirty pots we typically saved for cleaning at home. But we finally looked at a watch, and it was only midnight! We couldn't go home because we would look rather foolish. So we decided to wait a while, sitting against our packs.

We obviously fell asleep after having had so little sleep earlier. I vividly remember waking up at some time and seeing Rod sound asleep propped up against his pack. At daybreak we left for home. I'm not sure if we ever admitted to our parents how foolish we had been.

That was the last campout at the top of the hill. After that we moved our campsite down to the wide space next to the creek, which ran three feet below. Thus, we didn't have to worry about the water seeping into our campground. We were near a big old beech tree and the boundary line of the next farm, part of which is now Chadds Ford Winery. Thus, I can say I grew up in wine and ski country—quite a stretch. Sometime during those years, we felt compelled to stake out our territory, and the beech tree still shows the scars of our initials (F M, B R, R R and A M). The carvings are more than sixty-five years old but marred by a crude phrase added by some vandal years later.

A root of the beech had been eroded out from its surrounding soil and made a convenient step down to a small sandy spot where we could dip out water from the creek. Now here is a silly anecdote. Just up the creek, beyond the boundary fence, the water was very shallow and ran over rocks for several yards before coming to our dipping pool. Someone had heard that water running over rapids becomes purified. Perfect! We had ready drinking and cooking water. But remember, our campsite was down the creek from a working dairy farm; it was not a winery then. You can imagine what we were drinking.

When I mentioned this bit of nature lore to my father one day, he quickly told me in no uncertain terms that we were crazy and that from then on I was to carry a canteen and that we were to boil any water we used for cooking. I'm not sure how well sterilized our water was, but I'm here today writing this down. I also had to drink out of a swamp once, but I'll save that gem for the chapter about Hill Girt Dairy Farm, where I worked when I reached sixteen.

After that first farcical campout, we acquired a couple of pup tents, as they were called, perhaps from one of the army-navy stores that used to sell all sorts of military equipment left over from the war. A pup tent consisted of two heavy canvas pieces that buttoned together with the sides staked out. They were held up by wooden poles just tall enough so that a person could crawl in, sit, and lie down to sleep, with room for two people inside. Pup tents were heavy when rolled up, nothing like the big, lightweight nylon tents of today and certainly nothing you would want to carry on a trail hike.

Our one-night camping trips usually started in the late afternoon, following a swim. After all, there wasn't much to do at the campsite but sit around and talk. After supper we would pick black raspberries in the patch in our back pasture or get mulberries from nearby trees for our morning cereal, which came in small, wax-paper-lined boxes made by the Kellogg's Company. But at night there was something more interesting to do every now and then rather than sitting around talking: raid an apple orchard!

Getting to the orchard was quite a hike along the length of our back boundary, another field, and then beyond Baltimore Pike. Our goal, a small orchard owned by a University of Pennsylvania professor (like me), was a few hundred yards farther across the pike. Although we built the raid up in our minds as dangerous, we took so few apples that I am sure the professor would have said to go ahead and pick a few. But for young boys, doing something *dangerous* was a major attraction. Yet that same professor permitted Frank to set traps for muskrats living in his pond. Frank then skinned them and sold the pelts. I wasn't big on this activity, but I did go along to see the process at least once.

As we roamed the woods and the fields or swam in the swimming hole, I developed the ability to tell the time fairly accurately by the position of the sun, a talent I no longer have. We never wore a watch. However, if my parents wanted me to come home at a particular time, I would hear the sound of "Assembly" played by my father on an old Boy Scout bugle as he stood on our porch several hundred yards away.

Now I come to the real adventure of those years in the woods. The four of us built a ten-foot by ten-foot log cabin with a floor, two double-decker bunks, and a peaked roof, which allowed for a fifth guest sleeper in a loft—and no one ever took a picture! At least there are none in the family photo albums. We just didn't take many pictures back then with our Brownies, I guess. This is a real tragedy because the project was such an incredible effort by four boys aged ten to twelve when we began building. Thinking back over sixty-five years, it's difficult for me to believe it actually happened. Just as bad, I couldn't find a trace of it when I went back to the spot to see the ruins fifty years later; there was nothing showing above ground. Perhaps someone took the logs for firewood. But what happened to the boards that made the roof and floor?

The cabin stood proudly in 1947, though, after more than a year of construction activity. Bob was the engineer on the project, although Frank was still our leader. Rod and I were laborers. To start, we found some logs about two feet in diameter conveniently lying on the steep slope above our campground. Out came the big, two-handled crosscut saw that later saw so much action, with Rod or me struggling on one end and a bigger boy on the other. Back and forth, back and forth went the saw, a process that seemed endless until we cut through the long logs to create four of them ten feet long. Then, with long crowbars, we got the logs rolling down the hill to flat ground, where we placed them in a square at our campsite.

However, only two would remain on the ground. We had to cut in flat notches on opposite sides of each log (like those in

Lincoln Log sets) so that when we levered the other two up and placed them at right angles, they fit into the notches of the others, creating the foundation of the cabin. It was such hard work that I'm amazed we wanted to continue. What we had planned was an enormous project for us, and no adult ever helped.

We quickly realized that we needed a door, so we had to cut into the log we had just placed in the front to form the door sill. We then had to cut other, smaller logs shorter up to the height of the door, which must have been about five feet high. We then made a door frame from boards and did the same for the two sides to make window frames. For the window panes, we used big sheets of plastic; or possibly we scavenged two old windows. Then we *chinked* between the logs with clumps of sod to block out wind and rain, just as the early settlers had done.

All the logs, other than the four base logs, came from catalpa trees with trunks about eight to twelve inches in diameter. I'm not sure how we managed to lift the logs that fit above the windows and door, but Bob, our engineer, must have figured out something utilizing ropes. What is astounding is that the catalpa logs came from standing trees that we felled with our saw. I was detailed to ask my father if we could cut them down. He said we could as long as we stuck to catalpas. In these days of injury lawsuits, can you imagine that he didn't blink an eye when I asked? He would have blinked if he had seen athletic Bob once climbing up a tree hung up in other branches so that it was about at a thirty-degree angle, chopping away at the branches caught in surrounding trees with a hatchet until the tree he was standing on began to fall. Then he jumped off. Luckily all the other trees we cut down fell cleanly.

A big problem was getting some of the trees we felled to our cabin site. Some were close enough for the four of us to drag them, but others lay at quite a distance. What were we going to do? As luck would have it, a boy named David had moved into the house associated with the barn we had played train; and he had a horse that pulled a wagon. His father had been a fruit-and-vegetable peddler; and the horse, named Frank, was retired. David wanted to go to scout camp but lacked some equipment. So we *rented* Frank, his collar, and traces for the week in exchange for some of our camping gear. At the end of the week, we were pulling one of our relatively small catalpa logs with Frank when David came over to trade back. "You're making Frank pull that?" he exclaimed. When he met us, we were almost at the cabin site, where he then saw the huge bottom logs and said—I can still hear it today—"Come on, Frank, we're going home!"

Before returning to the construction story, there is one more humorous incident involving David and his horse. After the cabin was finished, we invited him and a couple other boys to camp with us. David arrived with Frank pulling a wagon that was covered with cloth painted blue from the set of a play at our school, which he had scavenged from the school dump. The wagon looked like something out of the Old West. We slept in the cabin, and our guests, in the wagon. The next morning we all hitched a ride in the wagon because it had started to drizzle. The problem was that the blue on the cloth was water-based paint. You can imagine what we and our gear looked like by the time we got home.

Now back to the cabin and the search for boards for the peaked roof, the floor, bunks, and the *guest* loft. A man living a half mile away on Baltimore Pike had an old chicken house full of junk he wanted to get rid of. He said if we could remove the junk, we could tear down the house and take the boards. So the band of beavers, if not brothers, did just that. The Russo boys' mother had a car trailer that we filled first with the junk and dumped. Then we tore down the building and loaded the boards into the trailer so she could haul them down to the creek on the dirt road leading from the barn. From there it was about two hundred yards to the cabin. We had to carry all the boards of course.

With the boards we built a peaked roof, the front and back ends under the roof, the floor, door and window frames, bunk beds, and the loft. For mattresses, we tore up an old mattress for its innards. During the winter, we found that mice liked our beds too. We finished off the roof with tar paper that we had most likely scavenged. Now that the cabin has vanished and with no photos to document its reality, I realize that it could have been like Briga-doon, a legendary village that appears for only one day every one hundred years, as depicted in a stage play and a 1954 movie. But the cabin was solid reality once.

There is a poignant story that ends my experience in the woods. When I was sixteen and my companions were no longer around for camping, I was one merit badge short of being an Eagle Scout. Ironically, what I lacked was the merit badge for Pioneering, which was required in those days. I had only to construct something out of wood, using ropes to lash logs together. My project was a bridge over the creek, but I kept putting off that really simple job. Then Dad said he would sit and keep me company while I constructed the bridge. Thus, one Saturday afternoon, there I was alone with my father in the midst of silence, when just a few years before shouts and laughter had rung out from the band of beavers.

CHAPTER 3

THE SWIMMING HOLE

The swimming hole was the only place to be on summer afternoons. If it was too cold, we would work on the cabin. But after we had finished building it, we were always swimming. The creek widened just below the wooden bridge in the dirt road that went from Farmer John's to our barn. Our pool was a section about four times the width of the creek in general. It was probably five yards wide and seven yards long, and its depth varied according to what the latest storm might have done to scour out the bottom or fill it in some with silt. After a big storm we always hurried down to see how deep the water was. Usually it came up to our chests, thanks to the dam we had made out of rocks and sod. Of course, the dam had to be repaired now and then, but this was simple for log-cabin builders.

The depth of the water didn't stop us from perfecting shallow dives from the bridge. Luckily we didn't break our necks. Rob, of tree-riding fame, was the only one who would dive from the railing rather than the floor of the bridge. One glorious day, though, we found that the depth was almost over our heads after a particularly violent storm; for a while during that summer we had much better swimming. With time and storms, though, the creek bed filled in again; and we were back to shallow diving.

Because we four were the only ones swimming most of the time, we were skinny-dippers. Once we got caught when two girls who lived on Baltimore Pike appeared suddenly, forcing us to stay in the water and make it cloudy by stirring up the bottom with our feet. But the girls rarely came so we had the hole to ourselves most of the time and didn't have to bother with swimsuits.

Then tragedy struck. We arrived one day only to see that the dam had been breached, which lowered the water level considerably. But we repaired it and all was well. It happened again, though; and this time we found two young mothers with their very small children in the creek. They were the dam breakers. We let them know that this was not the way things were handled, and there was no more trouble from them.

A true, serious tragedy did almost happen. The two girls who had surprised us earlier had a younger brother named Petey, very small for his age because he had a heart defect as I recall. One day Petey almost drowned in front of our eyes. We had found a big box that would float with one of us inside it. I was lazily paddling around in the box when I looked over the side and to my horror saw Petey's face just below the surface. He couldn't swim and had walked in over his head. His eyes were bulging, so he looked like a little tadpole. I quickly tipped over the box and pulled him to safety; and because he had only been under a few seconds, no harm was done. Funny, I can't remember any fuss about saving someone from drowning. It was just the thing to do.

Unfortunately, the month of August presented a problem for my mother. She was somewhat uneasy about my being in the pool during that month. Why? She was deathly afraid of my getting polio, or infantile paralysis as it was frequently called. She had been struck with the disease when she was a small child, leaving her with a partially withered left arm. Others who had survived polio were not so fortunate, because if their breathing muscles were paralyzed, they were condemned to living out their lives in an iron lung with only their heads sticking out. Alternating pressure within the rigid iron lung did the breathing for them. Imagine living in such a condition though. Some survived for many years, trapped in the iron lung. Horrible! No wonder my mother was so afraid.

Actually, there was no danger for me because the issue was swimming in a crowded pool, not an isolated creek. The polio, or poliomyelitis, virus could easily be passed on to another person in a crowded pool, but common folk had no idea what was causing the disease. In some people's minds, summer water was the culprit. Yet, in the early years of the twentieth century, scientists had discovered the virus and later worked on developing a vaccine. In the 1950s, a vaccine finally became available after careful testing. That vaccine required an injection, but soon scientists developed another, safer vaccine that could be taken by mouth. I remember getting it—a pink liquid on a sugar cube—with my wife and our two small boys in 1962 when there was a big community vaccination program. But our three children who arrived later received the vaccine as infants. Thankfully I never experienced the fear every summer that my poor mother did.

My mother entered the picture regarding the swimming hole on one other occasion. There were some nice warm days one March that just demanded to be taken advantage of, although she told me to stay out of the water for fear that I would catch a cold. In spite of those orders, on March 4, 1946 (according to the autobiography I had to write for my tenth grade English class), Rod and I plunged in. The water was shockingly cold, so I didn't stay in for long. Then I got the bright idea to put on my jeans to be warmer in the water. It's hard to imagine that I was stupid enough to come up with that idea because I was quickly as cold as I had been when naked. So I took off my jeans, wrung the water out as best I could, and laid them out in the sun. That did a bit of good but not enough to fool the sharp eye of my mother. She was a softie, so punishment was only a few sharp words. I had let her down though, and that was my real punishment.

To swim in a real pool was a dream. The Sunday school picnic, the Fourth of July (with fireworks), and Labor Day were the times we had that thrill. We went to Lenape Park, an amusement park that was about four miles from home and had a great big pool. It was such an attraction that one day Rod and I pedaled his bike over to the park and back, taking turns pedaling and riding on the cross bar. The pool even had a high diving board as well as the usual low board. When I was thirteen or fourteen, I got up the courage to dive from the high board rather than just jump. Gaining confidence, I graduated to doing Tarzan dives, which were done by running out to the end and then flinging myself out as far as possible with a big yell. Now I would be afraid even to walk on the board.

We had other fun at the park, foolish fun. We liked to get on the merry-go-round without a ticket and then jump off to avoid the ticket taker. Later, when my wife and I took our own young children to the park on Sundays before it closed sometime in the 1970s, I found that they had wisely put up a guard rail around the merry-go-round, with only one gap where the ticket taker stood. The fun house was always an attraction, so much fun that one time we decided to become part of the exhibit. We would stand behind a corner and then jump out to frighten the customers. I don't remember how long we did this before being rousted out.

Labor Day ended with the park and the swimming hole closing because we were forced to go to school. As we four boys left Lenape Park that night, we would say goodbye to each other with the standard comment, "See you in prison tomorrow." Deep inside, though, I was excited at the prospect of getting my new school books; but I would have never admitted it.

Those wonderful summer afternoons in the swimming hole finally had to end when Frank went off to work and Rob and Rod moved away. However, my father sprung for membership at Brinton Lake, just a few miles away. There I could perfect my freestyle swim with his help, but only on weekends. I guess I went to the swimming hole alone until the summer I was sixteen, when I could drive and was eligible to work on a big farm on the Brandywine. It was good to get out into the world finally.

CHAPTER 4

THE BARN

When our *pool* closed for the season and our camping activities ceased, the barn became our playground. It was a two-level, bank-style barn; that is, it was built into the side of the slope that ran down to the little valley behind our house. The barn's big doors opened at the level of our road, and the stables were in the lower level. The upper level had a broad open area with hay mows on either side.

Hung from a rail that extended the length of the barn at the peak of the roof, a big hay fork was attached to a pulley with a long rope reaching to the floor. In the days before the baling of hay, farmers would bring the hay in loose in a wagon. Then they dropped the fork into the hay, pulled the fork up, and someone dragged the large clump of hay over the hay mow and released it. A hole in the floor allowed for the delivery of hay to the animals in the stable below. Near the peak of the roof in our barn, there was a platform at the top of the open barrier that helped hold back the hay; and this was a great source of fun.

The first winter after our arrival loose hay gathered by a tenant farmer was still in the mow. As a result, my friends and I spent many a weekend afternoon jumping into the hay. We had to climb a ladder to the top in order to launch ourselves into space, landing in the soft hay. What fun we had! But that ended when the tenant farmer left and the hay disappeared. The hole in the floor to the stables remained, of course; it served as a neat escape route to the stables when we played tag throughout the barn. We managed not to get hurt engaging in these activities.

The barn was there for us to get hurt in, though, and corncobs provided the opportunity. We had a lot of field corn for feeding the animals, and we had to remove the kernels from the cobs. There was an old machine that did the job. We would place the ears of corn at the opening of a little chute, and then they fell into blades that rubbed off the kernels as someone (typically me) turned a big wheel that moved the scraping blades. The corncobs came out the other end.

They weren't wasted, though, because corncobs were a fine source of ammunition for an indoor version of a snowball fight.

But corncobs are light, so for long-distance battles we had to weight them. Water was the obvious solution. A soaked corncob is heavy, and throwing them at each other was crazy because they obviously hurt if they hit a target. I still remember the day when Rod and I were secured behind a big box during a pitched battle with the two older boys. We would stand up and throw, then duck down behind the box. Once I stood up to throw and caught a heavy cob in the middle of my forehead. That was it for corncob fights.

Later, we put up a basketball hoop in the barn and played half-court games, but bouncing the ball on a very uneven floor made dribbling difficult. When I was by myself before reaching my teen years, I made believe I was Tarzan by swinging on the old hay fork rope, launching myself from a big box and letting loose with a Tarzan yell. I was quite a fan of the Tarzan books; so receiving them as gifts for birthdays and Christmas was a real joy.

A few years ago, I picked up one of my old Tarzan books and began to read. I realized then that these books are really science fiction seen from the adult side of things. So I still read them and have even bought those that were missing from my boyhood collection.

As time passed, so did those childhood games, although turning the wheel on that infernal corn-shelling machine didn't. The animals still had to be fed. But I had an even more unpleasant job in the barn: plucking the feathers off the chickens that my father killed. I took no part in chopping their heads off, but my job was still unpleasant. To loosen the feathers so I could pluck them without tearing the skin, I had to soak the dead chickens in hot water, making them rather stinky. Worse, though, I had to pluck them in the barn, often at night when it was spooky being all alone.

The barnyard extended out to the right behind the barn, and beyond it laid the start of our ski hill. Frank had a pair of skis with rather primitive bindings that clamped our toes to the skis. We shared the skis and had a lot of fun going down the hill while others used their sleds. It was just straight down the hill on the skis until we came to a stop on the flat ground in front of the small creek that started at our springhouse. But my skiing days ended in a rather ridiculous fashion one afternoon when I was about fourteen. My parents had given me a pair of skis for Christmas, which I had to use on my own because the gang had begun dispersing. One afternoon I had the misfortune of running into a frozen pile of horse manure, breaking the binding on one of my skis but luckily not my leg. That ended my skiing because it wasn't much fun out on the hill all alone anyway.

On the other hand, a beautiful experience ended my time of playing in the barn. My Aunt Jean had taught me how to raise baby birds that had fallen out of their nests, although I'm not sure if most of them ever made it into the air. One did, though. Perhaps when I was sixteen, I found a squab that had fallen from its nest in the barn; and I began feeding it white bread soaked in milk. The little bird thrived on this diet, and soon I began to give it the finely ground corn that we fed our chicks.

As my pigeon grew, I introduced it to regular chicken feed. Then when it began to flap around on the floor, I gently threw it a couple of feet into the air to help it learn to fly. Next I let it fly off the big box I had used for my Tarzan stunts. When it was really able to fly, I began to tap on the wall to direct it to where I had put feed on the floor. After a few days of that activity, I realized that the time had come to release my pigeon outside. Pigeons were always flying around the barn, and my pigeon joined a group after I released it. The next day I tapped on the outer wall, and to my great joy it left the flock flying overhead and came to me to be fed. What a thrill! I repeated this procedure for a couple of days, and my young friend came each time. Then one sad day, there was no sign of my pigeon in response to my tapping; it had joined the wild.

CHAPTER 5

A WILD RIDE

I began dreaming about owning a horse from the time we arrived on the farm. Often I dreamed that I actually had one and was so sad to wake up and realize it had only been a dream. I kept plaguing my father to buy a horse, but he thought I wouldn't take care of it and that he would have to do the horse-related chores. He had good reason to think this because I wasn't the most eager of workers. But weeding a garden or cleaning chicken houses were hardly exciting jobs, I said. Taking care of a horse would be another thing. That argument didn't convince Dad. He was right, though. I was too young to have a horse of my own.

Instead of having a horse to ride, I read books about children who did. The first was Mary O'Hara's *Thunderhead*. It was a thrilling story about a beautiful white stallion, the son of Flicka, the star of O'Hara's earlier book, *My Friend Flicka*. The action took place on a ranch in Wyoming. As a teenager, I turned to books by Will James about cowboys and their horses.

Reading these last books made me dream of being a real cowboy. Indeed we had real cowboys from Texas on our land. They worked for a Texas cattle dealer, S. B. Davis, who rented our land for the last couple of years we lived there. He even had a corral on Baltimore Pike near our school where they put on shows. During those years many steers were brought to our part of Pennsylvania to be fattened for market on the lush bluegrass pastures of our region. The famous King Ranch in Texas even established a large spread about ten miles from us.

Finally, my father bought us a horse named Rocky and Western-style riding gear. He thought I would be safer in a Western saddle with a pommel to hold onto. But I soon found that it was just easier to climb on and ride bareback. Despite Dad's requests that I use the saddle, I never did. Mimicking the cowboys I saw frequently, I fashioned a cowboy hat out of an old Boy Scout campaign hat and always wore my jeans and jean jacket. I wasn't totally authentic, however, because I rode bareback like a Comanche. I just loved the feel of Rocky's shoulder muscles as he galloped beneath me; sitting in a hard saddle is not the same thing.

Now I will tell you three horse stories of my own that match those in the books I had been reading during those long years I went without a horse. The first ends with a choice I made that shames me still; the second is about an exhilarating ride but also illustrates how times have changed over the more than sixty years since it happened; and the last is of a ride on Rocky that almost ended in severe injury to both of us.

During the summer of 1946 when I was ten, I had to leave the cabin building that we had just started to stay with my grandmother in West Philadelphia for a few weeks. My mother needed a break from living with her mother-in-law on our side of the house while my grandfather was remodeling the smaller part that the tenant farmer had vacated. During that period, which was before the white flight to the suburbs, there was a mixture of white and colored—as I was taught to say then—families living in my grandmother's neighborhood. Thus, there were plenty of African-American kids around to play with, and I found one who made a great playmate. One Saturday my new friend and I went to a matinee at a movie theater frequented by African-Americans only. So there I was like a light bulb with my blond hair and very freckled white face in a sea of darkness. It was a great show, and I remember enjoying it very much. There was a sad separation of races then even in the North, which lasted far too long and continues in some ways even now.

But that's not the full story; and writing it now, more than sixty-five years later, still makes me feel bad. Around the corner from my grandmother's house lived a family that had a stable housing some ponies. I met the two boys who lived there, and they took me in to see the ponies. Well, I couldn't stay away from the place. One day their grandfather came into the stable and said quite sternly, "If you want to play with my grandsons, you'll have to stop playing with those n———." I was shocked and can remember looking up at that grizzled, ruddy face, thinking to myself, "What makes you better than them?" I'm proud to think I had that thought as a ten-year-old boy but am ashamed that the ponies tipped the balance. Oh, if I had only walked out when the grandfather made that ugly demand and not abandoned my other little friend!

Moving on to something pleasanter, I'll tell you about my camping trip in New Mexico that involved a lot of horses. At fifteen I was old enough to go by train with other boys from the Boy

Scouts' Chester County Council on a camping trip to Philmont
Scout Ranch in northeastern New Mexico. Never having traveled
farther than South Jersey, I found it difficult while looking at a
map to imagine I would soon be so far away from Chadds Ford. We
were to debark in Raton, New Mexico, after two days' travel, the
second night of which would be on the train known as The Super
Chief, which left from Chicago.

While riding in the observation car, we lost our seats in the regular coach to those who boarded in Kansas City during the night.
It didn't matter because we just stretched out on the floor of the
car and woke up to see the astounding, empty flatness of Kansas
in the morning. Frank and Rob, who had gone to Philmont two
years earlier, had vividly described the Kansas they saw through
the train window as looking like a huge blue teacup lying on a flat
table. They were right.

We were destined for a seventy-mile trek over mountainous
terrain, and camping gear was not what it is today. The tents
were heavy canvas; the sleeping bags were also heavy; and our
packs were not much better than sacks. Therefore we required
a beast of burden to make the trek. Each crew of about ten boys
was issued a burro, which we learned to load up each morning
and care for during the trip. All of this was arranged at a base
camp called Ponil.

Ponil had quite a few horses and burros as well as several big,
ornery, and dangerous draft mules that packed supplies to other
base camps scattered over the ranch. A young wrangler cared for
all this stock. You can guess where I spent as much time as possible
during the few days we stayed at Ponil: at the corral with the wran-

gler. Indeed, I was there enough times to earn my Horsemanship merit badge.

One day we set off on a trail ride, one horse after the other, with the wrangler leading. After a couple of hours, we headed for a spot for lunch and also to water the horses. When our destination came into view about a quarter mile away, the wrangler said, "Let's go!" and took off at a gallop. I can still see myself following suit and mounting a low bank to pass everyone else. With a commodious Western-style saddle to sit in, a full gallop was easy. To this day I can still feel that ride.

A few days into the trek found us hiking down a wooded mountainside, switch backing as we descended. From around the next bend, we could hear a loud racket: a lot of hee-hawing and angry shouts. Then the commotion stopped, and a cowboy arrived in view riding a rather stocky horse, leading a string of those huge draft mules hitched in a line carrying supplies. We stood in awe of the man, who told us as he rode by that the mules had begun to kick up a fuss and he'd had to "straighten them out." How he managed this I don't know, but the thought of it still impresses me.

We'll leave Philmont after another tale that illustrates how changing times have removed some of the excitement from boys' lives. Let's fast forward thirty years to 1982, when an older me was a scoutmaster leading a group of boys over the same ground I had covered as a boy. We had light, modern gear so there was no burro to manage. As before, our first camp was at Ponil; and there was a trail ride as well. But this time the ride consisted of a couple of hours plodding along in single file at a walk. At the end of the ride, I had great difficulty getting off my horse and straightening up after sitting so long in the saddle with no change of position. Obviously views of safety and liability had changed over the years. I'm not criticizing this, but that day I was glad I had been a boy in an earlier era.

Before telling you of the ride that came within inches of disaster, I want to mention the most exciting books I began reading when I was a teenager. They were in a series featuring the Black Stallion, an Arabian who could run like the wind. Many years later, when I was over fifty, I actually met Walter Farley, the man who wrote the books I had read as a boy. A young boy like me at the time I read the books, Alec Ramsay, owned the Black. There were a number of books about that beautiful horse, the most exciting of which involved the Black, who was never given a regular name, and his son, a red stallion. Everyone thought the red son to be faster than his father, so to settle this they scheduled a match race. But a regulation race never happened. Instead, the two were unofficially matched up, with only the Black having a rider—Alec riding bareback—as they raced down a mountain to escape a forest fire. The ride was exciting; I was so happy that my hero, the Black, won.

Now for the wild ride that I had on my own *black stallion* when I was seventeen and only a few months before I had to say goodbye to him. It was a race, too; but in this case the opponents were a group of Western horses. Rocky won in amazing fashion.

He had supposedly been trained as a jumper; but I had had no formal riding lessons and could never get him to jump anything. That changed, though, the day I decided to visit the small herd of horses belonging to the Texas cattle dealer, who also rented the neighboring farm owned by Farmer John. A barbed-wire fence with a Western-style, barbed-wire gate four feet high spanning the road separated the two farms. The dealer's horses were grazing on a hill on the other property, so I went through the gate, closing it after me, the proper thing to do. As it turned out, it would have been better to have left it open. We went up the hill to the horses, but only a few minutes after we reached them, Rocky began to act nervously as the other horses gathered around us. I realized I had made a mistake and decided we would be wise to leave. We trotted away; but then the herd of about ten followed us, streaming down the bank on the side of the road leading down to the barbed-wire gate.

Rocky then took off at full gallop toward the gate, which was about a quarter mile away. Roughly one hundred yards from the gate, it was time to slow down; but Rocky had other ideas: he was a runaway. He had the bit in his teeth and was in charge. The next best thing for me to do was to dive off onto the long, soft grass that edged the road on either side, which would have cushioned my fall. But luckily I looked back and, to my horror, saw that the galloping herd filled both the road and the verge on either side. With no other option, I buried my head in my arms, expecting that we would be wrapped in barbed wire within a few seconds. Then I realized we had cleared the gate, leaving the herd screeching to a halt on the other side and Rocky and me unharmed. I had not felt the jump at all. It would be nice if someone had been there with a movie camera, but in my mind I can see it as clearly as when it happened sixty years ago.

Of course I never dared tell my parents for fear they would ground me because of my foolishness, not to mention because I could have been seriously injured. What is amazing, though, is that I never told the story to anyone. I didn't brag to my high school classmates or tell my five children what their dad did when he was a boy. It was such a frightening experience that apparently my mind had just buried it. Then, about thirty years after that wild ride, I happened to be talking to a veterinary student and, as I usually do, asked where her home was. She told me that she lived in Chadds Ford on Hillendale Road, which was the road next to the field where Rocky and I began our escape. I replied to her, "Let me tell you what happened to me near Hillendale Road."

From that moment on, I became a firm believer in repressed memories, those memories that are buried because of some overwhelming horror—the image of me wrapped in barbed wire, for example. Wouldn't you think a father of five children would have regaled them with what Dad did? Telling it to them and other adults now, which I can't stop doing, is really not as much fun.

Thanks to Rocky I became a veterinarian. One winter morning I saw him limping a bit as he came across the pasture in back of our barn. I think he must have tangled with those Western horses and slipped. In any event, I told my mother that I wasn't going to school that day so I could nurse Rocky. That experience—fortunately things turned out well for Rocky—and working on Hill Girt Dairy Farm made me realize that veterinary medicine was for me. I never changed my mind later to study human medicine as so many of my college friends were planning to do.

CHAPTER 6

OTHER ANIMALS

After Rocky the topic of this chapter will seem quite tame, although there is some humor to it. Wait until we get to the *bombardier* hen! Rocky gave me many hours of pleasure; but we raised other animals for food, which was quite important to us. Caring for these animals took a lot of work; however, eating their products was quite a pleasure, too. Most of our other animals were chickens. In addition we raised a couple of pigs every year for their meat. Also, at one time or another, we kept a goat for milk and a sheep, Mary, who really didn't do anything. Maybe my father had visions of shearing her, but that never happened.

We raised both egg-laying hens and males for meat. My father sold the eggs we didn't need at the office where he worked. Indeed, the back seat of our car often contained several egg cartons as well as garden produce when he went off to work. The male chickens were one of my 4-H projects every year. 4-H is a youth development program started in the late 1800s to encourage young people to pick up the new agricultural practices developed in state universities, which their elders did not readily accept. Our club was sponsored by a local Grange, an organization established to foster agriculture. Those in the 4-H club were also members of the Junior Grange.

The little male chickens were *caponized* (neutered in dog and cat terms) by the county agricultural agent, who made a little slit in the side of a bird to access the body cavity and snip off the internal testes. Caponizing the birds made them much tenderer for eating a few months later; those caponized birds gave us wonderful chicken dinners. Thus, we never ate turkey at Thanksgiving or Christmas because my chickens were so much tastier.

But caponizing little roosters-to-be so that their meat would be tender is a thing of the past. It used to take a few months for them to reach a size for eating. Now selective breeding and improved feed has hastened the growth so the birds are ready for market as broilers, at least, in a matter of weeks. They remain tender even though they are sexually intact roosters.

A mystery surrounded those little birds soon after the caponizing process. Some of them would puff up on the side of the slit as if there were a balloon inside of them. We referred to this air under the skin as wind puffs. My job was to puncture them with the corner of a razor blade to allow air to escape. I never understood why this happened until years later when I studied the anatomy of birds in order to teach it to veterinary students.

Birds don't have expandable, movable lungs like ours; they have rather rigid lungs with tubes that pass through them. Branches of the tubes expand into thin sacs that extend through the body cavity and even into some of the light, hollow bones. This arrangement greatly increases surface area for transfer of oxygen into the blood. If the air sacs are damaged, air can escape from the body cavity, which results in the wind puffs I eliminated as a boy. The punctured air sacs obviously quickly healed because the wind puffs didn't reappear.

We kept the laying hens in a house that had nest boxes and a series of raised perches where the hens slept at night. A platform under the perches received their droppings, which reduced the manure that collected in the straw litter covering the entire floor of the house. When I was strong enough, probably around thirteen, Dad handed me the job of scraping the manure off the platform into a wooden bushel basket. The hard part was carrying that heavy basket to the nearby garden for spreading the manure. Dad's idea was that I would spread it over different parts of the garden, which was immense; and I tended not to stray too far from the henhouse, I confess. This subterfuge went undetected until the year we set our tomato plants near the henhouse. Manure contains a lot of nitrogen, and nitrogen stimulates growth of greenery. You can guess what our tomato patch looked like that year::it was a lush jungle of towering tomato plants. Fortunately, we did get tomatoes among all the greenery, although I heard about it from my dad.

I might as well get the rest of the garden story out of the way now. I don't shine in this one. I hated to weed, which was a major chore in the summer. Every morning I came down to breakfast to see the inevitable little memo from my father listing what I was supposed to do that morning from 9:00 a.m. to noon. I can still see his crabbed handwriting, which too often said to weed this or that part of the garden. I might spend other mornings picking strawberries in the rather large strawberry patch or picking black raspberries in the wild patch in the back pasture. Everything was *large* from my standpoint. Picking the raspberries was a pleasure, though, because I could easily eat some as I picked. They were delicious, and I still prefer the black ones to red raspberries. Often there was a big purplish stain on the front of my shirt because I would stop off at the patch on the way home from the woods to eat raspberries. Their thorns aren't nearly as vicious as those of black-berries, so the picking was easy.

Weeding was the big bugaboo, though, and the source of annual embarrassment to me. Once my little brother, who was about five, came to help me weed and then went crying to my mother, telling her that I was sleeping, not weeding. Every sum-mer I had to face the visit from the county agent and my former fourth-grade teacher, a stern lady who served as the director of our 4-H club. My project was always contaminated with too many weeds so I had to live with the shame and never really got it right.

With the garden out of the way, let's briefly return to chick-ens and the bombardier hen. When you entered the henhouse, the two tiers of nest boxes were to the left on the same wall as the door. A couple of yards in front of the nest boxes, we had a bucket of water for the hens to drink. Normally we opened the door quietly and slowly in order not to startle the hens. One day, though, I entered the house much more abruptly than I should have. Startled by my sudden entrance, one of the hens flew out squawking and flapping her wings from a nest box. (Chickens can fly short distances.) Unfortunately she happened to be just releasing her egg as she flew off. The egg flew through the air in a beautiful arc and dropped unbroken into the water bucket. Just like my jump with Rocky, that would have been worth a movie clip.

Another 4-H project were the two pigs we raised each summer, which weren't very interesting; and I was annoyed by the work I had to do for them. This consisted of carrying feed and water, including our kitchen garbage, to their pen in the apple orchard about two hundred yards from the house every day. At least we didn't need a garbage man with the pigs slopping up the garbage I carried to them.

Our goat, Meg, provided me with more fun than the pigs did, for sure. She was a beautiful white, friendly goat carrying a couple of kids inside her when we bought her. A goat isn't like a dog, though, so she really wasn't an animal to play with beyond petting her. However, the night she gave birth to twins was very exciting. My father kept going out to check on her; and when he came back to say that there were two little guys added to our goat *herd*, I rushed out to see them. There they were: a black-and-white male and a white female just like Meg; what a feeling that was to pet them. I named them Tomahawk and Flicka, the latter name being inspired by *My Friend Flicka*, of course, even though she wasn't a horse. I probably got the name Tomahawk from a horse in one of my Will James books. In a couple of months, though, Tomahawk was living up to his name and was very lethal with visitors. On the dreaded day for checking my gardening project, Tomahawk took aim at my former teacher and plunged into the cab of her pickup truck as she was getting ready to drive away. I apologized but found it very amusing to say the least.

Much more amusing, though, was training Meg to stand calmly on a platform with a wooden stanchion to hold her head that my father had constructed so we could milk her. We had already weaned her two kids, so it was our turn to relieve her of her milk. The first day we got Meg onto the platform, Dad tried to milk her from behind, which upset Meg no end. Luckily, Frank, Bob, and Rod had come by to watch the proceedings, and we all had to help. Each of us held onto a leg as Dad milked—another missed movie shot. Meg quickly calmed down when she realized, I imagine, that she was feeling better without an udder full of milk. My parents turned her milk into very good cheese because there really wasn't that much for drinking.

We sold her kids and later Meg when she no longer produced milk, and I was sorry to see them all go. I don't know why we didn't breed her again and have more fun with kids and eat delicious cheese. Probably Dad had more than enough work to do. After all, the farm work was in addition to his regular job in an office.

A funny group of animals, a flock of turkeys that belonged to the McFaddens, periodically showed up on our property; it was always fun to see them. Their turkeys, raised annually from little poults for marketing at Thanksgiving and Christmas, wandered freely but not far from their food source at the turkey house. Every now and then, the big bronze birds would come gobbling over from Frank's. I can still hear the goofy "gobble, gobble, gobble" sound they made as they wandered around. Of course they were closed in at night to protect them from foxes or weasels on the hunt.

If weasels get into an open chicken or turkey house, they will senselessly slaughter the birds right and left. Blood seems to be a powerful stimulant to them, just as it is to sharks. I saw the results of a weasel's visit to the McFaddens' chicken house, not a pretty sight. But chickens are no angels either. You may have heard the term "henpecked." Well, if chickens see another chicken with a wound that bleeds, they will gather around and peck the wounded bird to death and cannibalize it—henpecked takes on new meaning in such cases.

One domestic animal I feared and detested (and still do) is the honey bee. We had some hives, but only my father worked with them. In order to subdue bees, one can blow smoke in their *faces*. When Dad began beekeeping, he tried to produce smoke by puffing on one of my grandfather's pipes. Not being a smoker, he became woozy and had to find another source of smoke. Consequently, he bought an apparatus that would hold burning material—dried grape twigs worked well—and had a bellows that could pump smoke through a spout. Problem solved.

To call our bees domesticated is a stretch because we had a wild hive living in the wall of our house. Periodically the current queen bee would leave our house with a large group of worker bees, forming a swarm. The trick was to capture the queen and surrounding worker bees without getting stung. Dad scooped them into a box with sheets of wax covered with little cells, where the bees would deposit pollen that ultimately became honey.

We kept the bees within a small apple orchard near the pig pen.. Once when I was watching my father working with the bees, some bees began to buzz around me so I took off running. I ran as fast as I could, but one bee was hot on my tail because I could hear it buzzing close behind me. After about thirty yards I realized it was clinging to my shirt and not chasing me so I ripped off the shirt to get away. Silly me!

I've told you some exciting and funny stories about animals, but now I'll bring up one that is rather sad. Our gang of four was walking along our boundary fence in the back pasture one day when we approached the big dead tree where turkey buzzards often roosted. Not far from the tree, we came upon the remains of a dog that had been tethered to a bush. It had been shot and left to the buzzards. We recognized the collar as that worn by the dog belonging to the tenant farmer who had rented the farm land

and barn during the first year we lived there. His dog had tended to chase his cows, a no-no around a farm. Something had to be done to prevent this, and this was his crude method. We were very angry, of course, because he could have given the dog away. Obviously there was nothing more to be done.

Luckily our dog, Tootsie, an English/Gordon Setter mix, arrived after the tenant farmer had left. I say this because Tootsie ran everywhere and seemingly tirelessly. Barbed-wire fences couldn't slow her down because she took them at a jump, but not over four strands as Rocky did. Rather, she just sailed effortlessly between the lowest two strands. This turned out to be a bad idea, though, when she was nursing a litter of puppies. She was hanging a bit low then and once came home with a tear in one mammary gland. I shudder to think of it, but the tear was not big and healed rapidly.

Recalling the terrible incident of the tenant farmer's dog reminds me of another instance of an animal doing what it shouldn't have. That animal was my beloved Rocky. One day I was standing on our back porch and saw Rocky, whom I had put in the very large pasture in back of the barn, standing way up in the corner of our property. Not far from him, a small herd of Black Angus steers was peacefully grazing. Suddenly, I heard a trumpeting whinny from Rocky, and then he started running right toward the cattle. They took off like a shot, with Rocky behind them. Rocky had started a stampede! I could only stand and watch helplessly as the whole group ran the quarter-mile length of the pasture, only stopping when they reached the boundary fence at the end. Why Rocky did this I don't know; but I can't believe he thought, "Let's have a bit of fun with these guys." More likely he had been stung by an insect, or a car horn had startled him. Whatever the cause, I could have been in serious trouble with S.B. Davis; but as luck would have it, I was the only one to see the stampede. Again, it would have made a great movie.

The small, part-time farm I have been describing had many companions just like it, but they were quite a bit larger, usually a few hundred acres but with similar practices as far as the way animals were kept. After World War II, though, things began to change. Farms became much larger, and most animals are now kept in some sort of housing. Some decry this as cruel, but the issues are complex and difficult to discuss in a small book. I have done this in another book, *An Odyssey with Animals*, so I'll just mention a couple of things.

Today you don't see as many dairy cows roaming a pasture as in my day. If hundreds or even thousands of cows were kept out in pastures, they would trample their food supply. Thus, the grass is brought to them. Dairy cows have nothing to do but eat, drink, and ruminate (chew their cuds). Thus, a large, airy barn offers them all the room they need.

Something I miss in particular, though, are the many fawn-and-white cows of my boyhood grazing in the fields. They were Guernseys, and Golden Guernsey was the name people used in marketing their milk because the milk had a rich, yellow color due to a special substance in it. Now, most of the dairy cows you might see grazing are big, black-and-white Holsteins. They produce large volumes of milk with less butterfat content, which is valued in modern times. But the farmers handling cows now are no different, just more efficient so they can make a living.

Ending this chapter primarily devoted to animals with a passage from one of the books I read as a boy and mentioned earlier seems quite appropriate. For some reason, a conversation from *My Friend Flicka* burned itself into my mind. It illustrates beautifully what our relationship with animals should be, even on large, modern farms. We are the only species capable of caring about the welfare of other species, either individual animals or an entire species. Some ignore this responsibility of course.

In the following passage, rancher Rob McLaughlin is speaking with one of his sons about a wild mare that had broken loose from their corral with the noose of a lariat around her neck.

"What if it did choke her?" asked Howard. "You always say she's no use to you." "There's a responsibility we have toward animals," said his father. "We use them. We shut them up, keep their natural food and water from them, that means we have to feed and water them. Take their freedom

away, rope them, harness them, that means we have to supply a different sort of safety for them. Once I've put a rope
on a horse, or taken away its ability to take care of itself,
then I've got to take care of it. Do you see that? That noose
around her neck is a danger to her, and I put it there, so I
have to get it off."

CHAPTER 7

MID-CENTURY LIFE

Having talked about my playground and our animals, I think it would be interesting for you to know something about life in general during the years covered by this book—1944 through 1953—which were quite different from today. Of course World War II had a big effect. Beyond having relatives fighting either in Europe or the Pacific, civilians underwent the hardship of rationing of such items as food and fuel until June 1947. Even so, this was nothing like the misery of those in Europe, China, and ultimately Japan. In England rationing didn't end until 1955. As a young boy I wasn't really aware of these issues to any great extent; although when I was 10 or 11, I recognized that we were being deprived of a vital staple: bubble gum. It was in very short supply, so scarce that we tended to save it overnight for chewing the next day.

Strangely enough, another thing that sticks clearly in my mind is margarine, or oleomargarine as we referred to it then. It was developed in the early 1800s at the behest of Emperor Louis Napoleon III as a substitute for butter to be used by his army and the lower classes. Margarine was originally made from plants and animal fat, but the latter was dropped during the Depression and World War II. My striking memory is that, by law, margarine was white to distinguish it from butter and therefore protect butter producers. But spreading a white, oily substance on bread or other food wasn't very appetizing, so manufacturers did a clever thing: they put a red pill inside the wrapping so that the consumer could knead the package until the oleomargarine looked just like butter. We no longer have to do this of course.

We civilians contributed to the war effort by cleaning and saving all our tin cans in flattened form. Depending on how many tin cans a kid turned in at a collection center, he could be awarded an army rank, even up to general. And one fine afternoon in the fall of 1944, we were released from school to collect milkweed pods in the fields for the manufacture of life jackets. The kapok often used was from trees grown in the Caribbean and Central and South America; thus getting the kapok from there would have been difficult during the war.

My father was rejected for military service due to a spot on his lung. The closest person in my life who saw World War II combat was my second cousin, Bruce, ten years older than I. I once overheard my family telling a story about Bruce, who was fighting in Europe. The story, as I understood it then, was that he had been surrounded by German soldiers and was hiding behind a big rock. This was in late 1944, so he had been in the Battle of the Bulge, although I didn't know it as such then.

Perhaps twenty-five years later, Bruce and I were standing in the garden of one of my aunts after Easter dinner. I abruptly said, "You know, Bruce, when I was a kid I remember hearing a story about your being surrounded by German soldiers." Then I looked up at him—he was about six feet three—and saw that he had shut his eyes and lowered his head. He was shaking his head slowly from side to side, saying nothing. Oh, how sad and stupid I felt. Having studied aspects of posttraumatic stress disorder (commonly called shell shock or battle fatigue back then) later in my career as a sleep researcher, I should have known better. I suspect he probably had flashbacks and nightmares about that experience so long ago.

PTSD, as the disorder is commonly referred to, is a terrible affliction that some cannot escape after being part of, or seeing some awful event they cannot control, such as that associated with combat. The lingering effects can be so terrible that some are driven to suicide in order to escape.

To learn in May of 1945 that the war in Europe was finally over was great, but there was still Japan to go. Then that summer the war ended with the dropping of atom bombs on Hiroshima and Nagasaki. The enormity of those horrible events didn't really have a big effect on me because I only saw a couple of pictures in the newspaper. We didn't have television to view the effects of the atom bomb over and over again.

My interest, however, was in what an atom was, so I asked my Aunt, Jean. When she told me that a piece of wood was composed of atoms made up of nuclei with little things called electrons whirling around them like the planets circling the sun. I couldn't believe it and still have trouble picturing this. I then began to think that maybe we were inside an object like a giant piece of wood and on and on *ad infinitum*—not a novel thought I am sure.

Instead of the world becoming perfect as my youthful naïveté would have it, we shortly acquired a new enemy: the Soviet Union, our former ally. Not only that but my youthful mind also had to deal with the beginning of the Korean War (while I was at the Boy Scout Jamboree in Valley Forge) and a horrible new bomb that outdid the atom bomb: the hydrogen bomb. Because of this threat, we went through safety drills in school that consisted of crawling under our desks for protection should the Soviet Union launch such a bomb. We would have been protected from falling debris but nothing else.

The threat was so real to me that once when we were out in the country at the cabins owned by my mother's family, I was feeling very safe and happy. Then I happened to hear a sound and looked up to see a big plane flying high overhead, and that destroyed my nice feeling of safety. I can still picture exactly where I was standing and the direction in which I was looking when I saw that plane

However, life was still fun in spite of these vague threats. But what was life without television? Few had TV sets in their homes. My grandfather finally bought one in 1950 that I could watch. Also, some neighbors with TV sets were willing to allow others to come in to watch a show. Thanks to this habit, we kids spent many a Saturday afternoon watching cowboy movies in our neighbor's living room.

It wasn't really a problem living without television, though, because there were radio and a boy's imagination, with the pictures in comic books of some of the radio heroes to help. (What man of my generation hasn't thought that he could be rich if only his mother hadn't thrown out his comic book collection, these rare items being sold now for great profit?) Every weekday afternoon from five to six o'clock, I was glued to the radio listening to my programs, which were each fifteen minutes in duration. At various times there were *Terry and the Pirates*; *Jack Armstrong, the All-American Boy*; *Buck Rogers*, a spaceman of the future; *The Green Hornet*; and *Superman*. All combatted crime and evil of course.

One of my favorite programs was *Captain Midnight*. He headed the Secret Squadron, charged with fighting international crime and espionage. A World War I hero, he received the name Captain Midnight from his commanding general after having carried out a very important secret mission at the stroke of midnight. The radio show ran from 1938 to 1949 and then showed up on television for a couple of years in the early fifties when I was in college and no longer interested.

Now for the punch line: I was a member of the Secret Squadron! How did I manage that? Well, I had to wait until my mother bought a jar of Ovaltine, the sponsor of the show, at the beginning of the year. I then mailed in the proof of purchase seal found inside the jar. For this important yearly act, I received a membership card, a manual with the year's code, and a codagraph that allowed me to construct secret messages. These could only be decoded by a fellow member of the Secret Squadron. Every year I waited and waited for my codagraph to arrive in the mail. (I saw on eBay that I could be selling those things for $150 had I been smart enough to keep them.)

Strangely, my fellow squadron member and friend since fourth grade, Johnny Aaron, always received his membership materials many days before I did. This was annoying so I finally asked him how he could be so lucky. "Oh, I don't wait for my mother to go to the store," he told me. "I just go into the general store across from my house and open up a jar to get the proof-of-purchase seal." Of course the jars were not sealed in those days. As a result, he didn't have to wait for his mother to buy a jar as I did. When I reminded him of this slippery act a few years ago, he countered by noting that he *did* leave behind the jar filled with Ovaltine. But what if my mother had happened to buy *that* particular jar?

Another top program was *The Lone Ranger* (*the Masked Rider of the Plains*). Astride his horse, Silver, and accompanied by his faithful Comanche companion, Tonto, he fought against evil in the West. The Lone Ranger reached me weekly in the evening; I can remember lying in bed in the dark listening and imagining the Lone Ranger's adventures.

One of the best parts of the half hour was the introduction, which still can thrill me as I remember the stirring words spoken by a deep voice: "Return with us now to those thrilling days of yesteryear, when out of the past come the thundering hoof beats of the great horse Silver. The Lone Ranger rides again!" I also loved the accompanying music, the last part of the *William Tell Overture* by Rossini, an Italian composer of the early nineteenth century. And, silly as it seems, I was as thrilled at seventy-six as I was more than sixty years ago when I listened to the program's introduction again, thanks to the Internet. (Johnny told me that it was listening to that music that inspired him to become a lover of classical music. I, on the other hand, love the music of bagpipes–not appreciated by everyone.)

While lying in bed at night, I also listened to the *Grand Ole Opry*, beamed to me from WWVA in Wheeling, West Virginia. Because of the way radio waves bend at night—I don't remember the physics of this—I was amazed that the program could reach me from so far away. Not only could I listen to country music, but various farm-related commercials reached me, such as the one advertising baby chicks for sale. Imagine this today!

Learning that some of my programs would move to television, I was really excited. *The Lone Ranger* transitioned well, for it was really another cowboy show and easily looked realistic. But what a disaster *Superman* was in my eyes. Without the tricks that computers can play and without color television, when Superman flew he was just a guy in a gray, shabby costume, looking as if he were suspended by hidden wires. My imagination was much better.

Now, I see our mid-century high school as a rather innocent place. We didn't have the plague of drugs as far as I knew. The most outrageous vice was carried out by a couple of guys who sneaked gin into their lockers at school and showed up to class a bit tipsy. Of course those were the days of hot rods with dual carburetors competing in dangerous drag races. Thankfully, I didn't have a car that could compete. In fact, the most dangerous thing I did with a car would be nearly impossible today.

We had a 1940 Ford station wagon, which we used to drive around the farm once we had purchased a used 1949 Stude-baker—the car that looked as if it had two hoods. The electrical system of the Ford had given out, but we saw no need to repair it since we didn't have to drive the car at night. Driving on the open road during daylight hours presented no problem. But I forgot about the lighting problem one evening when visiting the home of a girl living a couple of miles away, and I had stayed until dark. What could I do? I had to get home, so there was nothing to do but drive home in the dark. At least there was some moonlight, as I recall. One additional problem: more than a mile of the drive was on Baltimore Pike, a very busy, four-lane highway today. In 1952, however, the Pike was a three-lane road, as were most major highways then; and the Pennsylvania speed limit was 45 miles per hour. Thus, I made it home safely peering at the lane lines and, thankfully, meeting no cars in either direction.

The Studebaker and my sixteenth birthday released me from the farm and traveling on a Trailways bus to reach the bright lights of Kennett Square six miles to the south, which was home to my high school and other delights. One activity that led to yet another ludicrous experience would not have been so easy without that precious driver's license, which allowed me to be away from the farm on my own. Three of us had formed a little band. Harry Kevis was a drummer, who told us his father had played drums for

Tommy Dorsey, one of the more famous of the big bands of that era; I played the trombone, although not well because I didn't like to practice; and Bobby Maucher played the accordion—a rather old accordion. We just fooled around at Harry's house on Saturday afternoons, recording our efforts on a tape recorder.

Then we mentioned what we were doing to friends and received an invitation to play at the Saturday dance held at the Snack Shack in Kennett Square. For our first—and only—gig, we added another instrument, not a sax or a clarinet, but another trombone played by an older boy. Fortunately we had the accordion for the high notes. Thinking we were very clever, we billed ourselves The Snack Shack Trio Plus One, rather than the more prosaic Snack Shack Quartet.

Although Harry was a very enthusiastic drummer, he had one problem: he tended to pick up the beat as a song went along. When we got to the first—and last as it turned out—fast song, The Snack Shack Trio Plus One ran into trouble. As the song progressed, the tempo increased; and the dancers had to struggle to keep up, as did the accordion. When the song ended, the dancers came up to us sweaty and mad as hornets; and Bobby's old accordion had blown a gasket. Suddenly we were finished—for the evening and as a band. I can't remember what embarrassment we faced at school on Monday, but years later Harry's widow assured me that he had learned to keep an even tempo and was good enough to play with jazz artists Stan Getz and Chet Baker.

Those were relatively innocent times: times I sometimes wish would return.

CHAPTER 8

CHADDS FORD SCHOOL

Have you ever wondered why a seemingly inconsequential thing will stick in your mind for years? You know from my story of Rocky's jump that a powerful, negative event can bury itself in your mind; but other small events may pop up every now and then, really silly things. One of these memories comes from the beginning of my years in Chadds Ford School. When I was in fourth grade in September 1944, we began our study of geography, one of my favorite subjects, with Baffin Island in the out-of-the way Arctic. It sticks in my mind that the book was brownish and probably eight and one-half by eleven inches in size. Why of all places on the globe would Baffin Island appear front and center in the geography book right off the bat? It's hardly central to the world's economy. But as I think of it, the lesson to be learned (deliberately or not) was that everyone didn't have a life just like mine, that our customs and environment were not necessarily special. This is not a bad thing to learn when you are young, and the topic clearly made an impression on me.

I would have made an impression, though not a good one, on my classmates in my new school had I shown up wearing knickers. Instead of long pants, we wore knickers with long stockings in more urban areas and at the suburban school I attended until we moved to the farm. We also wore white shirts with ties that fastened with a band around our necks. Initially I wore the tie and white shirt as a newcomer in Chadds Ford, but with long pants at least. After some argument I managed to convince my mother that the tie was not the uniform of the day in Chadds Ford. However, no arguments were ever persuasive enough to send me off to school in blue jeans—never.

Now for another one of those silly occasions that were a part of my formative years. Did you ever paint yourself into a corner, figuratively speaking? Well I did early in my career at the school and never really escaped until I went away to college. Not far into fourth grade,

I proudly announced that I had been born in Scotland. While regaling the class with this false gem, I looked up at my teacher. She said nothing, but her stern visage is still clear in my mind. She brooked no nonsense, but for some reason she let me prattle on, perhaps waiting for one of the other kids to call me on it. No one did, and somehow my nickname became Scotchy. John says it was the girls who came up with it. (The word "Scotch" is now a reference to whisky so that a more appropriate nickname might have been Scotty.) That nickname stuck through high school: it was on my sports jacket, and even appears in our senior class yearbook. Even one of my high school teachers always called me Scotchy, and one of my old friends from high school , Wanda Kevis, sometimes does just to tease. But until now, I have never revealed this secret from sixty-odd years ago.

What caused me to enter that corner in fourth grade? Indirectly, my Aunt Jean did. She loved all things Scottish because my great grandfather had brought his family to America in the late nineteenth century from Scotland. Jean made me a kilt with all the trimmings when I was about five, and I had a record of bagpipe music that inspired me to march around imagining I was a Highlander.

She also had a book, *The Scottish Chiefs,* with stirring pictures that I pored over as a little boy; and she filled me with stories of Scottish heroes William Wallace and Robert the Bruce. The edition of *The Scottish Chiefs* we had was illustrated by the great N. C. Wyeth, who was mentioned in the preface. *The Scottish Chiefs,* published in 1810 by a modest Englishwoman, Jane Porter, is regarded as one of the greatest historical novels ever written. It depicts the First Scottish War for Independence from England at the turn of the fourteenth century . Led by William Wallace, the Scots fought against the Viking-Normans of King Edward I, who had already defeated the resident Anglo-Saxons to the south.

Clan Morrison originated as far north as one can get in the Outer Hebrides, the tip of the Isle of Lewis. Legend has it that a Norse ship foundered in heavy seas, leaving survivors to make it ashore. Hence, there is Scandinavian blood in the Morrisons, including a tiny bit in me presumably. But this all happened long ago in the thirteenth century.

Although this account sounds romantic, life was harsh for ordinary folk in Scotland. For example, my great grandfather was a coal miner near Glasgow, as were his older sons. Ultimately, they emigrated from Scotland to Pittsburgh and the mines there when my grandfather was twelve. Although my grandfather also entered the mines then, he left at thirteen to become an apprentice glassblower. Despite this more recent harsh heritage, the love of Scotland was embedded in me, embedded enough for me to tell that whopper proudly. I also have a very soft spot in my heart for miners due to the discomfort and dangers they face, but I'm very grateful not to be one of them.

In addition to the proud announcement of my Scottish background, I made another big splash in fourth grade. I was the top magazine salesman of the entire school, which went up to the tenth grade at that time. My grand total in magazine sales was fifty-six dollars, the highest in the school; folks were amazed at what a good salesman I was. Of course they didn't know that my mother and four doting aunts had bought all those magazines. My aunts were either unmarried or childless at the time; and my brother was just an infant; thus I was king of the hill. It was a one-shot deal, though, because those subscriptions were multi-year naturally. Obviously, fourth grade was a banner year for me, even though I faked it a bit.

Stepping aside from my very personal history for a while, I would like to speak about a bit of important American history related to Chadds Ford. I do this in part because Revolutionary War soldiers likely passed through the farm on their way to the Brandywine Creek and Chadds Ford, where the Battle of the Brandywine took place. Our school lay next to the fairly wide Brandywine, where this pivotal battle in the American Revolution took place. Thanks to the schoolteacher/devoted historian Chris Sanderson, we learned all about the Battle of the Brandywine in a school assembly on the anniversary of the battle, which took place on September 11, 1777.

Due to insufficient knowledge of the countryside, General George Washington just missed being encircled by his British opponents. They and their Hessian (German) allies, led by Sir William Howe, had sailed from New York and landed at the northern tip of Chesapeake Bay, aiming for Philadelphia. Washington's army met them along the way north but ultimately settled down for battle north of the Brandywine in Chadds Ford and its surrounds along the creek. The reason for this placement of his troops was that the Brandywine was the last defensible position between the British and Philadelphia, twenty-five miles away.

Howe split his force about four miles from the Brandywine, sending one contingent to confront Washington directly at Chadds Ford and the other to the west. Washington thought he had all fordable places in the Brandywine covered; but farther to the northwest, where it has two branches, there were places to cross unknown to him. Thus, although prepared to meet the British and Hessians head-on at Chadds Ford, Washington had to reorganize his troops quickly when he finally learned that a large detachment of enemy soldiers was approaching on his right. Washington received this information from Squire Thomas Cheney, a judge, who had seen the flanking British army crossing the ford unknown to Washington and rode at a gallop for five miles to warn him—Chadds Ford had its own Paul Revere.

Ultimately the colonials had to retreat, but they were not destroyed and lived to fight another day outside Philadelphia. But along the peaceful Brandywine on that day in September, the battle resulted in five hundred casualties on the British side and twice that number in Washington's army. Can you just imagine those colonial, British, and Hessian soldiers possibly walking on the fields of our farm on their way to Chadds Ford all those years ago with such a terrible day ahead of them?

Chris Sanderson, who told us about the battle at our school assemblies, was quite a character. He had a radio show during which he spoke of his beloved history; he went to every presidential inauguration from Teddy Roosevelt to Lyndon Johnson; he roamed the countryside collecting historical artifacts, which are exhibited in the Chris Sanderson Museum in Chadds Ford (Johnny Aaron is now a docent there); and he was a fiddler with a band, The Pocopson Valley Boys. The band played at wedding receptions and the like as well as for square dances.

Occasionally, square dances were held at the school on Saturday evenings, and Chris called the dances as he led his band. He was a crotchety old guy, who brooked no nonsense on the dance floor. If one of the adults didn't do the dance correctly, Chris would stop the music and march right down from the stage to instruct the hapless individual who had attracted his attention. In spite of this rough behavior, he was very gentle with children.

Chris also liked to announce the presence of those who were not of the community and have them raise their hands. Thus, regulars would let him know about a visitor in the group. At one dance, Johnny and I took a chance and sent a note up to the stage saying that friends were visiting from Alaska. Chris announced that there were visiting Alaskans, but no hands were raised. I can't remember his reaction, but we got away with that little trick.

We were boys and were mischievous at times. The most common infractions in class were fooling around or talking to another person when we were supposed to be listening to the teacher. If one stepped over some line in the teacher's head, it was out to the hall to serve the sentence, standing there looking like a fool if anyone walked by. The really dreaded punishment was the command, "Go up to Mr. Haldeman's office"—in other words, the principal's office. There were rumors of a big paddle, but I only received a strong talking-to the one time I can remember being there. Nevertheless, the memory of that event is fixed in my mind because the waiting was worse than the punishment. Mr. Haldeman's office was on the second floor at the end of the school facing the direction of the farm. I remember standing outside the office where I could look through a window and see the side valley off Route 1 that led to the woods and thinking, "Oh, I wish I were up there instead of here."

But these indignities were nothing compared to those suffered by the relatively few African-American boys and girls in the school. The first six grades of these children were grouped together with only one teacher. Ironically, their room was called the Union Room! Clearly their education could not match what we received from a teacher teaching just one grade. Before school and during recesses, however, we all played together; but then we separated when it was time to go back to class. When the African-American children reached seventh grade, however, they mixed with the rest of us in our classes. The few boys were also permitted to partici-pate on junior high school sports teams. As I look back, it was all a sad, despicable situation, but I don't remember recognizing the paradox when I was a student. What the logic of that arrangement was escapes me.

At last the African-American community had had enough, and the school was fully integrated in 1950 thanks to the pressures applied by the parents. That date sticks in my mind because my brother's first-grade class was the first to meet in the disbanded Union Room. Johnny reminded me that his father, who came from Tennessee, was president of the school board that had made the change, just a few years before the Supreme Court ruled that racial segregation in schools was unconstitutional, not to mention morally wrong. What amazes and saddens me is that I thought nothing about this situation. I thought it was just the way things were. But this hurt the African-American children, of course, as they told me several years ago at a reunion of our class of 1950. Indeed, only in the middle of the civil-rights movement of the 1960s did it suddenly hit me: I went to a segregated school!

This ugliness sat in the middle of my beautiful Brandywine Valley. In addition to the physical attractions surrounding me was another kind of beauty to which I paid little heed as a boy: the art produced by the Wyeth family. Oh, I knew of N. C. Wyeth through his illustrations for *The Scottish Chiefs* and other books of adven-ture, but the paintings of Andrew Wyeth didn't affect me then. As a young boy, though, I recognized the Wyeths when they showed up at our school on the square dance floor; however, it was as a young adult that I paid attention to art and recognized the greatness of the paintings of Andrew and then his son, Jamie.

What adds to the art for me is the fact that some of the paintings focus on boys that were in school with me, including Allan Lynch, who was in my elementary school class. Allan appears in a painting titled "Winter 1946," running down a hill wearing a black hat with earflaps. He is also the subject in "Young America," which pictures him sitting on his bicycle staring into the distance. Johnny told me he was the original owner of that bike, which he had received (second-hand) in 1943; he gave it to Allan when Santa brought him a bicycle (also second-hand) in 1946. Allan added the embellishments to the bike seen in the painting. Also, our ninth-grade class had a Halloween party in the barn belonging to the Kuerners, who were Andrew's friends and models for many of his paintings, as was their big white farmhouse. Indeed, my favorite painting is "Evening at Kuerners," in which the house stands to the side of the painting with one brightly lit room and their springhouse lying near the center. A copy of that painting hangs over my bed.

Thus, in those years I unknowingly lived and played among treasures, both the beautiful valley and the art that depicted it.

CHAPTER 9

HILL GIRT DAIRY FARM

I was forced to drink from a swamp my first day on the job at Hill Girt. The reason for such drastic action was that I was working in a big field under a hot, early June sun, loading fertilizer into bins on a spreader. After the bins had been loaded, the tractor driver, John—one of the parents who had worked to end segregation at our school—would spread the fertilizer down the length of the very big field. Nobody worried about water needs in those days; we carried none with us, which led to my desperate act. Fortunately a swamp with precious water was quite handy at one edge of the field. Thus, during one of John's runs, I sprinted down the hill to gulp up water and goodness knows what else to quench my desperate thirst. Before John turned the tractor for his return run, I made it back up the hill, and he never knew of my foolishness. Remember, though, that I had had earlier experience drinking from questionable sources while camping in the woods a few years earlier, and had survived that little adventure.

Hill Girt was a large farm for my area of the world , sited along the Brandywine about one mile down the creek from Chadds Ford. I believe several smaller, adjacent farms had been merged into one with the main farm. As far as I can remember, all of the milking was done on the main farm, while the others were used mainly for housing heifers or non-milking cows, growing grain crops and hay as well as storing them. The owners, the Haskell family, had a dairy (Greenhill) in Wilmington, where the Hill Girt milk and other milk was processed and then delivered to stores and even house-to-house. Of course home delivery of milk is now a thing of the past.

Being sixteen and having a driver's license had allowed me to get a job away from home and finally leave the cursed garden weeds behind. The funny thing is that I worked far harder at Hill Girt than I ever had at home. Funnier still is that I loved it.

Dean Belt, who was a year ahead of me in school and on the agricultural track in school, alerted me to an opportunity to work where he had a job at Hill Girt. Thus, one spring weekend I went to ask for work. The estate manager, a Scotsman named Mr. Dodd, interviewed me. When he asked me how much I wanted per hour, I was a bit flummoxed because being out in the world alone was new ground for me. Then "sixty cents" popped out of my mouth. How that sum came to mind I don't know, but Mr. Dodd accepted me on the spot. Maybe I had undersold myself, I thought. But later, my father said that the wage was okay and was impressed that I came up with something on my own.

Hill Girt milked beautiful Guernsey cows and even kept bulls for breeding. The latter was safely housed in a very sturdy paddock because you don't want to mess with a dairy bull. They are as dangerous as the notorious water buffalo. The cows were kept in two long rows at milking time, with their heads held in stanchions designed like the one we built for Meg, although these stanchions were made of sturdy metal. Between milkings, the cows were turned out in a pasture, except when there was bad weather. Then the cows stayed in their stanchions, but there was plenty of room for them to lie down in nice deep straw or sawdust. When indoors during icy conditions in the winter, they could spend their days contentedly eating, chewing their cud, or sleeping, just as cows do when in their pasture.

Let's take a minute now to learn some facts about cows and the process of rumination, during which they chew their cud. Ruminants, such as cows, sheep, and goats eat grass in all its forms (fresh, hay, or silage). They need help to digest it, however, because they don't have the chemical enzyme that can digest cellulose, a major component of grass: the helpers are microorganisms, bacteria and protozoa, which do contain the enzyme. Thus, these tiny fellows digest cellulose for the ruminant, which lives, in part, off their efforts.

Now I should clear up the misconception that cows have four stomachs. They have one large stomach with four compartments connected to each other. When cows eat, they chew a bit and then swallow; and the grass or hay enters the largest stomach compartment, the rumen, filled with previously eaten grass mixed with water and copious amounts of saliva. This mass resembles a large breakfast bowl of oatmeal; think of it as *green* oatmeal. The most recently eaten grass, being less dense, floats on the *oatmeal* until it is mixed in with the rest. Minute after minute, contractions of the rumen mix the mass, just as a washing machine agitates to clean clothes. The ingesta, which is the proper name for the glop found in the rumen, actually slops back and forth between the rumen and the reticulum, which is the next compartment and smaller than the rumen. The reticulum also houses the ruminant's little helpers. Because a gas is produced as part of the process in the rumen and reticulum, a ruminant has to eructate (burp) every couple of minutes or else it would bloat and even die.

When a cow is relaxed and not walking, it is usually lying down ruminating, unless it is sleeping. If you observe a cow chewing without eating, then it is working on the cud, which has been regurgitated from the rumen. After a bit of this, the cow swallows. If you look carefully for several seconds after it swallows, you will see another cud running up the left side of the neck, just like a mouse under a piece of cloth. Meanwhile, down in the stomach, ground up digested ingesta periodically passes via a small opening into the third compartment, the omasum, where excess fluid is absorbed. The partially digested food then enters the last compartment, the abomasum, which is just like our stomach. Here substances other than cellulose are digested by enzymes and acid.

When mature cows are out in a pasture, they do little more than walk slowly around to get grass to eat and water to drink, or they lie down to ruminate or sleep. Now, though, most cows are kept in barns, where they can walk around; but they still stick to the previously mentioned milking routine. Instead of walking around a pasture to crop grass, they eat from feed troughs. Two, even three times a day now, the cows march from their big house into a milking parlor to be milked.

The cow stands on a platform, and a milking machine is attached to the udder via cups placed on the teats so that rhythmic sucking draws the milk out of the udder, sending it on its way through pipes via vacuum into a holding tank. Periodically, a milk truck comes by to pump out the milk for transport to the dairy where it is processed and bottled. In much earlier days, a farmer had to milk by hand, squeezing the teats hanging from the udder to draw milk out and into a bucket, while the cow stood in its stall restrained by the stanchion. Then milking machines came along. Before the idea of a milking parlor was introduced, the farmer would carry the machine that had sucked out the milk to a refrigerated tank. I had this arduous duty a few years later on a farm in Maine, where my parents were then living.

In the days when cows were milked while in stanchions, the herd would amble in from the barnyard and each cow would peacefully go to its own place. However, there were always a couple of ornery critters that wouldn't obey the rules and had to be shooed into their spots. They seemed to make a game of it every day.

Sadly, I didn't get to milk those beautiful cows at Hill Girt; there were regular milkers for that task. But I liked to watch whenever I could get a free moment. My job was to help gather the food for the cows, which was hard, dusty, sometimes itchy work. In June we began filling the big, tall silo with wet, chopped grass, which was brought to us in big wagonloads. A couple of us would stand behind the truck, dragging the grass into a trough that fed into a blower extending to the top of the silo where the grass was blown into the hole in the roof. Hour after hour we would drag the grass into the trough with hoes, and every now and then we would pour bags of dusty, ground grain into the trough. This additive would mix with the grass in the silo and enrich the silage, which is fermented grass that provides some of the food for cows. Inside the barn was an opening that connected to the bottom of the silo, where the silage could be pulled out for the cows every day.

Silos can be dangerous places to be in when there is silage fermenting because the gases produced rob the air of oxygen. One can easily die in a silo if not careful—and not only by being gassed. Not long into my tenure as a silage maker, I was party to a near tragedy that turned out to be funny when it was all over.

Unbeknownst to us, Mr. Grace, the farm manager, who could be crotchety at times, had climbed into the silo. He may have told someone he was going up to inspect the silage, but we at the trough didn't get that message. When a wagon came in to be unloaded, we began dragging grass into the trough and adding the dusty, ground grain to the grass. Not too many minutes later, a very dusty, very angry Mr. Grace appeared, shouting I don't remember what.

Luckily he was only dumped on by our initial effort, but that was enough to cover him with dust and knock his hat off, which was quickly buried. He had managed to scramble out before being completely buried by the load. Farms can be very dangerous places.

After filling the silo, we moved on to other fields to make hay. This was heavy work for those of us who had to load and unload the hay bales. After the grass was mowed and raked into rows, it was left to dry. Then the baling machine came along to form bales of hay wrapped with wire or twine, spitting them out of a chute toward the wagon that was pulled behind the baler. A couple of us standing on the wagon had to stack the bales; and this was hard work, even harder when the grass was alfalfa, which made very heavy bales.

We worked long hours when baling hay because it was important to get the hay in before rain hit the mown grass. If this happened, the grass would lose nutrients as it dried again. Because of the urgency to get hay baled and carted away to shelter, we always loaded one more time at the end of the day and brought the wagons in to the barn for unloading the first thing in the morning. Starting the day by unloading heavy alfalfa bales into the hay mow was not something I looked forward to. Now, however, hay is formed into huge cylindrical bales that no one can lift without mechanical help.

Sometimes horse nettles can infest a field of grass. While the grass remains edible, hay from such a field leads to misery for those handling the hay bales. Hill Girt had such a field, and I will never forget the day we baled there. Another boy and I were so itchy that at the end of the day we ran from the barn to a mud pond hidden mainly from view of the estate house, stripped off our clothes, and wallowed in the mud. We were so miserable we didn't care if anyone saw us or not. What relief!

The work was hard, but we kept our spirits up by joking much of the time. One who kept things lively was a guy named Shorty, who lived and worked around the village. He kept us laughing as we toiled away. Years later, I visited the Brandywine River Museum, which houses many works created by the Wyeth family. Much to my surprise, as I turned a corner Shorty appeared—not in person but in a painting, "Portrait of Shorty," by Jamie Wyeth. He sits in a chair wearing an undershirt and unshaven, just as he appeared when I worked beside him on the farm in 1952—but ten years older.

Although I wasn't entrusted with a tractor at Hill Girt—a big disappointment—I did become a dump-truck driver. One of my jobs was to collect garbage weekly, but better yet, to transport barley and wheat to one of the barns where grain was stored. This required certain finesse as the truck had to be positioned just right in front of the hole in the barn floor where the grain poured down. If the positioning was off, then there was a lot of shoveling to do. Obviously, the incentive to get the truck into the right position was considerable.

My most pleasant memory of that summer is when Dean and I once combined wheat into the evening hours, with him driving the combine and me following with the dump truck. For supper, Mr. Grace brought us pails of fresh, cold milk. That was enough. The field we were in was just a short walk to the Brandywine, where at the end of the day we stripped down and dove into its cool, tranquil water.

That was the summer of 1952. Although I did work on Saturdays during the school year, I thought I would be back full-time at Hill Girt the next summer before heading off to college. It was not to be: our family would be off to Wisconsin in June of 1953. My time in the Brandywine Valley was coming to an end.

EPILOGUE

"You really loved that place, didn't you, Adrian?" My brother said this one Saturday while I was visiting him. "Yes, I did—very much," I replied. Of course David had no close attachment to the farm because we left it behind when he was eight, my age when we arrived. He didn't have a group of playmates and the opportunity to participate in so many unusual adventures as I did, and he was too young to ride big Rocky.

For a long time, I had wanted to write something other than the many scientific papers I had written throughout my career. My first book, *An Odyssey with Animals*, satisfied part of my need, but it is still focused to a large extent on science. They say one should write about what he knows best; in my case this is boys. When my daughter asked me to write down stories I had told, I had the subject I knew best close at hand: me.

As I wrote, the memories flooded my mind; and I could see the events as they happened. I felt as if I had returned in time to a very enjoyable period of my life: I was a boy again, building the cabin, saving little Petey from drowning, teaching the pigeon to fly, and galloping on Rocky. We did some dangerous things, though, that make me shudder to think about as an adult with grandchildren in these modern times: felling standing trees and jumping over the barbed wire gate for example. Although I'm glad I had those adventures, I don't recommend following in my footsteps.

Along the way, though, other memories crept in and begged to be written down. Most of these provided a view of life in America during the early post-war years as the country was turning into a true super power and before television took over our lives. Some memories were not pleasant though: the threat of nuclear war—still a problem of course—and the forced separation of races. Others were fun to recall: that gig at the Snack Shack, lying in bed at night listening to *The Lone Ranger*, exchanging secret messages via my Captain Midnight codagraph, and playing train with manure buckets. These were simple pleasures, requiring mainly the imagination of boys.

Now, looking back over more than sixty years, I realize how truly fortunate I was, with fifty-two acres to play in and a horse to carry me like the wind.

46563646R00051

Made in the USA
Middletown, DE
01 June 2019